Football:

Pure Poetry.2

(The Return Match).

Selected & Edited by Ted Smith-Orr.

With the financial assistance of
The Professional Footballers' Association
& Pamela Blomfield.

Published 2002
CREATIVE ENERGY *cannot be measured by time spent at the workbench* **PUBLICATIONS, 365 HOLMESDALE ROAD LONDON SE25 6PN**

ISBN 0953429652

ACKNOWLEDGEMENTS.
We are grateful for the financial assistance of the **Professional Footballers' Association and Pamela Blomfield.** To Paul (Shoulders) Rodgers for information & covers. Brian Dann & Arriane Destiny for books. Purple Patch Poetry Convention, West Brom. Faber & Faber. Patrick Collins, The Mail on Sunday. Kelly Cauldwell, Random House Childrens Books. Cathy Marshall, Slamdunk Books. Adrian Mealing - Roger McGough & Ian McMillan. Adrian Mitchell. Ricky Rodgers, PC advice, again. www.footballpoets. David Thrilling. Roger Bing and Penny Smith-Orr, and my family, for their editorial expertise and for putting up with my enthusiastic ramblings. To others I have overlooked who gave help and support, as have many who submitted poems regardless of whether they have been accepted for publication.
We thank you all.

Some Poems have been published by:- *Faber & Faber,* Seeing Things, 'Markings.' *Random House Children's Books,* Over the Moon, 'The Game Or is It.' *Macmillan Books,* Collected Poetry for Children, 'Internationals' - Gareth Owen. *Puffin 2002,* Good Enough to Eat, 'I Have a Dream.' *Seren 95,* this house my ghetto, 'Famous Player.' *Shoestring Press,* Waiting for the Invasion 'Journey of the Maggies.' *Bloodaxe Books,* Blue Coffee, 'By the Waters of Liverpool.' *Others appear in the biogs at the back.*

Pre Match Pasta.

Welcome to the second edition of Football: Pure Poetry. The book is a
journey from the past up to this year's World Cup Finals in Japan and Korea.

Our poets include season ticket holders, fans, couch potatoes, programme and
fanzine poets, women, club poets, poets in residence, poets out of residence and a
poet without a residence. Two journalists, two ex professional footballers, one
playwright, several top professional poets including a recent Nobel Prize winner.

The poems are a roller coaster in time, starting in 1911, often reflecting the work-
ing man's game, with age and youth bringing us though the years. There are
poems about games in the backyard, Wembley and overseas.We meet personalities
as diverse as George Falconbridge and Zinadine Zidane.(Of course Mr Beckham
gets a mention). Managers and refs are some of the many subjects to be included.
As the poems progress they reflect some of
the changing attitudes, opinions and events from the past, through the luxury
years, up to the big crash in 2002.

There are poems to make you smile, laugh, cry, reminisce and remember events
you forgot or maybe never knew about. I have enjoyed every poem for the way
the poets have conveyed their stories in their style and voice. Some poems have
been given editorial assistance and everyone has been given the opportunity to
hone their poems to their satisfaction and your
enjoyment.

I know that not all of you read poetry and several of you get more from the
rhyming poems. I offer that you take each unrhyming poem as a small story
encapsulating the event described.You will be moved, at least, by many.

I hope you enjoy our book.

Ted Smith-Orr.
Poet / Publisher.

4

Contents.

Why is Football the World Game

Because you only need a Ball -
Any Ball! - Rag Ball -
Leather Ball -Tennis Ball !
Tin Can -Ball! Stone Ball!
Any Ball - Foot-Ball !
No Kit - No Pitch !
No Commerce ! Playing in
Backyard - Backstreet -
Playing in School-Time: Home-
Time -Lunch and Tea-Time!
Playing on Sunday.Birthday.
Deathday. Holiday. Seven -
Days-A-Week-Day!
Because - Anywhere in the
World.- You only need A Ball!

Dennis Gould

Football is

football down the alley-way football in the street
football for the whole wide world not just the elite
football under lamplight football on the beach
football with a rolled up sock football with a peach
football in the job centre football in the gutter
football in the superstore with organic butter
football belly-dancing football shiatsu
football when you're making love football on the loo

football with your budgie where the goals are small
football with a walnut instead of just some ball
football in the school yard shorts ripped and grubby
football when goalies wore green sweaters and were tubby

football when you're little football when your big
football down at B & Q football at a gig
football teams of boys and girls football in the shower
football with oranges or even elderflower

football for the very poor football for the old
football in a wheelchair or even up a pole
football with traffic wardens football with police
football in the Shetlands and in the Middle East

football in the duvet football under cover
football with the girl next door football with her mother
football with the tabloids your football or your life
football on the telly but don't tell your wife
football with a poet I hate it when they rhyme
But football with Gabby Yorath any flipping time.

Crispin Thomas
Chelsea

When Saturday Comes
(With appologies to Rudyard Kipling).

If you can keep your head throughout the season,
Although your team is losing games galore;
If you can hope, when there's no valid reason
To think this side of Christmas they will score.
If you can travel up and down the nation,
Through rain and fog and ice and deepest snow,
Returning home in utter desolation,
And wond'ring what it is that makes you go.
If you can show your goalkeeper no pity
Should he just let the ball slip though his hand,
Then minutes later chant a tuneless ditty
That your team is the finest in the land.
If you can shout and swear at the officials -
So blind and so unfair towards your team -
And tell them how to use their flags and whistles,
While doubts upon their parentage you scream.
If you can make the ideal team selection,
And think the manager is always wrong,
If you believe the board have earned ejection -
And you express your feelings in a song.
If you can chew the nails upon your fingers
For ninety minutes during a cup tie,
And all next week the winning goal still lingers -
But till it came, you thought that you would die.
If you keep programmes till they're old and musty,
And buy a strip each year (despite the cost)
If, when your team's won, you cheer loud and lusty,
And boo them just as loudly when they've lost.
If you can hardly wait for summer's ending
To see your heroes on the sweet grass run,
Soccer is yours! all other games transcending,
And - which is more - you'll be a Fan, my son !

Geoffrey V. Willis
Ipswich Town.

Sporting Superstitions

Got me rabbit's foot
And my special sock
And me dad's old shirt
And I'm clutching a rock
That I found on the terrace
When we won 6-0
And just before the whistle
I stand quite still
And count in reverse
From ten to three
Then turn and face the feller
Sitting next to me
And I shake his hand
With a special grip
And I finger me lucky
Apple pip
From the apple that I ate
When we won the cup
And I'm carrying my special
Library book
With the bookmark that's a feather
From a certain duck
And football's a game of skill
Not luck
Yes, football's a game of skill not luck

Ian McMillan
Barnsley F.C.
Poet in residence

Eye Test

AX
TOP
AXH

Referee!
You want your eyes testing.
Linesman!
That was never offside.
Penalty ref!
Oi, the ball was over the line.
Handball!
Off Off Off
Referee!

Ralph Hancock
Manchester City

Heroes

Although I'm older than my heroes
their young faces in old photographs
still look old to me.

Now I'm older than the faces in the photographs:
I'm more than twice their age
of nineteen or twenty three.

But today they are even older
In their seventies, maybe eighties,
I think of them youthfully.

They sit silent in their photographs
locked in youth for eternity,
but forever older than me.

Now I'm older than my heroes
of nineteen or twenty three
I repeat myself, quite frequently.

Because I'm older than my heroes
locked in youth for eternity.

Ted Smith-Orr
Charlton Athletic

You Can't Keep Poetry Out of Football

(Northampton v Gillingham 1997)

The steward gently pats me on my jacket
Exposing two bulges
A plastic bottle of Evian water
And the 'Best of Betjeman.'
Harmless enough in the real world
But in football stadiums
Water and poetry are considered dangerous
And must be surrendered.

But these searches never find every bit of poetry.

Listen:
The away fans have sneaked in
A rhyming couplet
"Can you hear Northampton sing?
We can't hear a fucking thing."

Some onomatopoeia -
"Push your shit aaaaaaaaaaaaaaaaaaout!"

Iambic Trimeters
"You know you are, you're shit."

Rhetoric
"If you want a goal - how wide?"

Hyperbole
"Gillingham F.C.
The greatest team the world has ever seen."

And nonsense doggerel
"There's only
One Stevie Butler.
One Stevie Butler
Walking along
Singing a song,
Walking in a Butler wonderland."

I swallow the water
Drop the bottle in a bin
Hand over the Betjeman
For safe keeping.

Through the turnstile I
Squeeze - the one undetected
Haiku supporter.

John Coldwell
Gillingham

Swindon v Barnsley 1911

I read in the Evening Advertiser,
How Swindon and Barnsley,
1911's losing F.A. Cup semi finalists,
Were invited to France that year,
To Le Parc des Princes in Paris,
To contest a match for a compensatory European trophy;
Swindon won 2 - 1, and some ninety years later,
The cup has just been re-found,
Doing service as a flower pot,
In a Wiltshire garden.
I was musing on this theme
Of the present re-inventing the past
As I walked through the the tunnel of the Swindon Railway Works,
And past the old watchman's hut.
It's a sort of re-painted sentry box,
The point where the watchman kept a check
And his eye on the thousands of busy railwaymen,
Hurriedly starting or ending their day
Though he never caught a man I knew,
The man who entered thin and left fat
After a day's hard labour:
Long lines of copper wire wrapped around his chest,
Bulging beneath his jacket and coat,
The raw materials for his sideline; electrical re-wiring,
Conducted profitably from his shed;
Or perhaps they just let him go,
Life was like that then,
Easy going.
Anyway, the watchman's hut is empty now,
There are no workers to check on anymore
But there is a small note pinned to the back of the hut,

And if you get really close you can read the tiny lettering,
"Smile, you're on camera."
It seems pointless to have a camera checking empty space,
But, I suppose if the watchman hadn't been originally there,
The camera wouldn't be there today:
The present recreates the past
And the past re-invents itself .
Now if only they could do that with the F.A. Cup,
Because at the moment it's neither use, nor ornament;
You'd be better off winning a flower pot;
And we have,
2-1,
In 1911.

Stuart Butler
Swindon Town

France 1914 - 1918.

A history tutorial, a student
spreading on my desk
all that had come back
from the trenches, her grandfather's watch
long since stopped at ten to three,
his pay book, King's Regulations,
a Royal Artillery badge
(an Arsenal man perhaps)
five Woodbines packeted,
never to be smoked.
Bryant and May, and on a torn off
scrap of card, the football results
from some long forgotten war time Saturday,
a stub of pencil the teletext of the trenches.
West Ham had won at home.
Blackburn Rovers held to a draw,
how much it matters and how very little too.

Ted Booth
Charlton Athletic

The King of Southend
(George Faulconbridge)

I was a confident kid
half blind in a hard time
and taught to expect nothing.
But I could dance with a football
and made men look fools
with a jinxing run down the wing.

My luck was in when the scout
had me spotted in the local league.
My old man signed the forms
and I sprinted to the station
to catch the first train south.

In that blue town
I was the one-eyed wonder
with more tricks in my boots
than Fred Astaire. I could dribble
twice round a daisy then lob the goalie.
No sweat. My name's in a book:
The King of Southend United.
Today I'd be a millionaire.

Sometimes the kicks of the past
shoot deep inside my legs.
When the pain's too much
I stay in bed and swear at the walls.
To pass the wakeful nights
I twiddle the radio knobs and try
to tune in nineteen thirty-five.

Derrick Buttress
Nottingham Forest

Markings

1

We marked the pitch: four jackets for four goalposts,
That was all. The corners and the squares
Were there like longitude and latitude
Under the bumpy thistly ground, to be
Agreed about or disagreed about
When the time came. And then we picked the teams
And crossed the line our called names drew between us.

Youngsters shouting their heads off in a field
As the light died and they kept on playing
Because by then they were playing in their heads
And the actual kicked ball came to them
Like a dream heaviness, and their own hard
Breathing in the dark and skids on grass
Sounded like effort in another world . . .
It was quick and constant, a game that never need
Be played out. Some limit had been passed,
There was fleetness, furtherance, untiredness
In time that was extra, unforeseen and free.

Seamus Heaney
Everton

Learning the Rules

Brotherly love

Hitting big David, aged five,
And making him cry
And run home to his mum,
Got his younger brother carried off the pitch
Shoulder high.
And it was forgotten
He didn't know which side of the line
The goalie should stand.

Finder's Teachers

I don't care if Douglas did find the ball first;
I got it.
No I wasn't sorry for throwing him over my shoulder
And I don't care if we both have to stand in the playground
All playtime.
But I think it's cheating
If you keep the ball.

Final Whistle

When our mums' called teatime,
Our mates took their jackets
And our goalmouth got miles long
And we always lost.

Ted Smith-Orr
Charlton Athletic

Sir Tom Finney

The sleeping giant
that roared your legend
again and again
with passion, muscle and vigour.
The warm warm embrace of the town
that flung open the gates
of invincible history
and the majesty held court
robed all in the lilywhite.
The original dream
of heroes
untarnished
did not splinter nor separate
such unimagined theatre,
Jesus rode home
on a donkey,
You,
you took the bus.

Catherine Marshall
Liverpool

England 3 - Hungary 6

nineteen fifty three:
at Wembley a devastation of those
slow heavy dancers
shown-up by poetry and ballet heralding
a dawn of glory
remember their names:- Ference Puskas :
Zoltan Czibor : Hidegkuti :
poets of
Hungarian Soccer Genius.
I never forgot one goal -
as the ball swings over from wing
Puskas takes it on his instep
swivels round, the ball still on his toe
flicks it onto his other foot
shoots!
a goal.....
a unique goal
in the entire history of this universal
teamgame : **Football!**
a Puskas goal at Wembley in nineteen fifty-three.

Denis Gould

The Cup Final of 1954

Looking up from the obituary
Of another goalless draw
You said:
I remember the Cup Final of 1954.

Turning down the noise
Of another dismal quiz show
You smiled:
We were the first to have a telly
In our street, you know.

We heaved it into the corner
And sat, proud as punch, on the settee.
You shook your head:
Everyone in the street crammed in to watch.
Everyone, that is, except me.

I'd switched it on early,
Then made sandwiches while it slowly warmed up.
You laughed:
Then I couldn't squeeze back into the room
And when I did - we'd won the cup!

Andrew Detheridge
West Bromwich Albion

Charlton Athletic v Huddersfield Town.
21 December 1957

It's Pete's first visit to the Valley:
Half time and Derek Ufton's in hospital;
and rumours of a steel pins in his shoulders - again!
We're cold ...miserable ...ten men and 1-2 down,
regretting having to play them again in the cup,
and unsure about inviting Pete.
Twenty eight minutes to go. It's worse: 1-5.
And there's about as much chance of bringing Pete again
as Trevor Edwards playing for Scotland.

A blur of blue and white stripes - of red
and one white stripe - that stripe's everywhere:
Stuart Leary's running - Don Townsend, upright-alert,
Fred Lucas is heading the ball to our team,
"Buck" Ryan stops blasting it over the bar-scores.
Johnny Summers is a bull; dropping his shoulder
turning and running at the goal - scoring.
"Who scored?"-"What's the score?"-"Who knows the score?"
No-one knows the score.
Someone tells Pete; "Shut up, you're over exited."
He knows the score: 4-5.-He screams louder.
Willie Duff is playing a blinder. Now he's not - now he is.
Billy Kiernan? No it's Ronnie White
thundering his small frame up our wing.
Summers, right foot: 5-5
Summers' right foot again- his fifth our sixth.
They'll never equalise.- We've won.
Hewie; own goal: 6 - 6 -we're frenetic.
This is our Valley, our cup tie - our Cup Final.
Our seventh-ìBuckî Ryan. Our game - our Christmas Day.
Our 7-6

As one - the terraces empty onto the pitch.
(A watch hits me, so precious, a man's weekly wage).
Cheering and chanting for Summers and Ryan, and Charlton.........

They emerge in the stand with Huddersfield's players,
speaking to us over the Tannoy... We can't hear a word.
"Hip, hip, hooray, for Summers and Charlton, and Huddersfield,"
we sing and we whistle. we clap and rattle our rattles.
Our heroes, our sportsmen. Our Team.

We replayed the game on the train,
in the pink and green Classified papers.
In The News of the World and Monday's sports pages.
Johnny Summers regenerated his career
and remains a legend,
at Charlton.

Ted Smith-Orr
Charlton Athletic

Bus Ride on a Rhyme with Burnley.

The first time I ever saw 'Town' versus Burnley,
Our keeper's name was Harry Fearnley.
If I remember it rightly, there were four of us,
Sitting with Denis Law on a service trolley bus.

No top of the range for Denis,
                        Unlike today's hero Clyde.
Denis was too young anyway,
                        So he joined us, for a council bus ride.
His fellow Scot's lad, Gordon Low
                        and Kevin McHale, as a rule,
Would ask, "How you gone on this morning?"
                        When we were playing for school.
We'd describe our game in great detail,
                        Today it seams so absurd.
These were three of our heroes,
                        Hanging on our every word.

Graham Shaw
Huddersfield Town

Danny Blanchflower

Cool as Sinatra
the loose - limbed
philosophical lines
pulled the famished heart
towards the natural light
of a brilliant sun that warmed
did not burn
forged a hole through defences
big as the canyon and poured
into it the riches of genius
that gathered in its shadow
the football soul that is love,
despair, madness, grief and joy
the joy that touched both
sides of the rainbow
with integrity, anatomy and glory
balanced as a cat on the wall.

Catherine Marshall
Liverpool

Collecting Autographs

When the football specials had steamed back west,
When the last faint gleams of terrace street sun
Slipped behind the shadows of the stands,
And the ground went abruptly quiet and numb;
When the crowd had made it's hot chocolate way home
And the terraces and streets were suddenly empty.
Do you remember the mayhem outside the players' entrance-
Do you remember collecting autographs?

Crowds of kids, scrap books and pens thrust upwards,
Huddled together by the red and white fence,
Hoping for names of star centre forwards.
Me with my scrapbook with pictures from all the
Sunday newspapers, stuck in with flour paste,
Of players, arms aloft with toothless grins,
In wintry darkness, mud, mist, rain and vapours.
But my best prize was to have my programme signed,
Open in the middle with teams in 2-3-5 formation.
If you could get all twenty-two to sign on their lines
In symmetrical pattern - such elation!
It gave me order out of chaos,
Form out of function, and a record of events.
You could file away reality
And you didn't give a toss
Whether you won, drew or lost,
For autographs were the real actuality.

Stuart Butler
Swindon Town

nine all and fifteen three

sad and strange echoes ring
pictures rise and fall
painful teachers drawn - out days
i can still recall
churning stomach walking in
homework never done
outside workmen joke and laugh
in snow and rain and sun

far away those echoes now
and long gone hymn filled hall
the magic bell of going home
and waiting for the call
and running crazy satchel flying
through the old playground
dribbling hurtling screaming stretching
bodies all around

fifteen, twenty, eight- a- side
no-one really cared
"you have him he's useless.."
life was being there
in worn out shoes with cardboard
playing in the rain
concrete pitch and shins all grazed
clothing torn again..

and after in the lamplight
up against the wall
tapping trapping all alone
my old tennis ball
and in that empty playground
trying hard to lose
growing fears of going home
mud - stained, ripped and bruised

and sneaking under turnstiles
soaked and wet clean through
dreaming dreams you cling on long
as only dreamers do
but who could dream this simple game
would swift outgrow us all
would crystallise to rule our lives
but is it still Football?

(....as we know it)

Crispin Thomas
Chelsea

daydreaming

what did you do at school today, son?
well dad, I had a good day;
we did spelling and writing,
and a maths test, nail biting.
.........and today I was up front for the Clarets,
although the conditions were bad.
I scored with a header
the volley was well in.
this boy of mine is soccer mad!
what did you do after lunch today, son?
well dad I had a good day;
we did science again,
it was hard on my brain.
.........and today I was playing for England.
my pace was electric
I scored a second half hat trick
this boy of mine is soccer mad.
what's that
you've brought home from school today,son?
well dad I had a bad day;
I was pulled by the ear,
given lines by the teacher,
who said in a very loud voice;
you've neglected your work lad.
as he stood there screaming
.........you were sat there daydreaming...
this boy of mine is soccer mad!

David Longley
Burnley

Grounded

Words I haven't used in twenty years
fall fluent and familiar as a mother tongue:
goal-hanging, nutmegged, offside trap,
turn on a sixpence, one two, a great touch.

Aged nine, in time to Sousa crackling on the Tannoy
I march off to the main gate,
selling programmes, duffel-coated,
gloved and scarved against the wind.
In the tea bar women emptied catering packs
of coffee, creamy clouds of fine dried milk
into a giant urn where it was watered,
stirred and alchemised
until by kick-off there was milky coffee
in a sky blue cup of perfect earthenware
warming up the cold curve of your hands.
Peas ladled into polystyrene cups,
mint sauce decanted
from the Cash and Carry jars
too big for me to even hold.

I ruled the sweet display
three-shelved, glass fronted.
handing over Wagon Wheels and Mars Bars
demanding money proudly
on the strength of my own maths......................

Out on the touchline for the ninety minutes,
the men in overcoats, the hopeful boys,
two players' wives, our full-back's mum and me
screamed out, "Man on" and all believed
that in a ground so small we were of help.

Eleven years of Saturdays
hands freezing to the rail
heart bouncing on that grid of lines and semicircles.
a template for elation and despair
indelible as poetry or catechism.

Nell Farrell
Eastwood Town
& Arsenal

Internationals

Lined up in the back yard
We both call Wembley,
Me and my big brother, who's twenty - two,
Pick countries:

What team you going to be then?
Can I be anybody?
It's your birthday, you can be anybody you like.
I'll be England.
I raise my fist and shout,
ENGLAND - ENGLAND - ENGLAND -
  ENGLAND !
Except England, he says.
You said I could be anybody.
Except England, I'm always England.
Why are you always England?
It's a 'rule'
Oh!

Who shall I be then?
You can be anybody you like.
Anybody? I'll be Brazil. Yeah!
I dance round doing the samba,
BRAZIL - BRAZIL - BRAZIL - BRAZIL!
Except Brazil.
Why can't I be Brazil?
Because I'm Brazil.
Who says?
The 'rule' says. I'm always Brazil except...
Except?
Except when I'm England. That's the 'rule'.
Oh!
Who shall I be then?
It's your birthday. Be who you want.
Anybody at all?
Anybody in the whole world...

I'll be Man U.
I jump in the air shouting,
MAN U - MAN U - MAN U - MAN U!
Except Man U.
Why can't I be Man U?
Because it's a club. Clubs don't play countries.
Who says I have to be a country?
The 'rule' says.
Oh!

Think of somebody else.
Anybody?
Anybody in the whole world.
But I can't think of any other countries.
You could be your school team.
Schools can't play countries.
Yes you can. It's a 'rule'.
Oh!

I'll be Weld Park Primary Under 9s.   Yeah!
WELD PARK PRIMARY UNDER 9s -
   WELD PARK PRIMARY UNDER 9s -
      WELD PARK PRIMARY UNDER 9s -
         WELD PARK PRIMARY UNDER 9s
So it's Weld Park Primary Under 9s v.
                              Brazil at Wembley.
And Weld Park score in the first minute. Yes!
Offside by miles.
Oh, come on!
Are you arguing with the ref?
Ref? you can't be Brazil and the ref.
Yes I can. it's a 'rule'.
No it's not

Yellow card for arguing with the ref.
Oh ref! Diabolical decision.
And it's the red card for Weld Park Primary Under 9s
Ah ref, you can't send off a whole team.
Yes I can. It's a 'rule'.
Oh!

Sitting in disgrace upon the bench
I ask him when do I get to make the rules.
When you're grown up and mature like me,
He explains,
Sliding home a winner
And dancing his victory jog around the flower beds,
While I make for my birthday cake
And an early bath.

Gareth Owen
Everton

Johann Cruyff

Moving like a sidewinder
as lethal
as deliberate
turning textbooks orange
totally...
the bridesmaids
more beautiful
than the bride.

Ron "Chopper" Harris

Traded with tackles so hard
they turned wine
back to water...

Catherine Marshall
Liverpool

The Save

Their left - winger chips Baz
and goes on a flyer down the touch line.
Steve tracks him, but he's shot it,
swears at Ade to cover his space.
The left - winger feints for the middle
then cuts back for the corner - flag,
which is okay by me.
Now I don't have to worry
about a direct shot on the run.
I'm skipping about on my line,
nervous because we're 1 - 0 in front
in the Notts Sunday League final.
Their useless strikers are hovering
just inside the penalty area
when the left - winger slips fat Col,
which is easy, he's so knackered,
wraps his left foot around
a beautiful cross.
But it's too far out for me
to leave my line, and it's flicked
on, anyway, by one of their strikers
into space on the right.
I'm on the wrong foot with that flick
so I see only a kind of blur,
which is their right - back who's legged it
pretty fast up the field to hit the ball
full on, dead centre, six inches above the turf.
It looks a certain goal the moment
his toe-end hits the ball...

only I twist and dive,
left arm parallel to the ground
and the ball smacks against my forearm.
It feels as though somebody's hit me
with a plank, but it doesn't matter
when the ball flies up
and over the crossbar leaving me
face down in the dust, totally winded,
and all the daft bastards
jumping on me and kissing me,
kissing me like they really meant it.

Derrick Buttress
Nottingham Forest

Gordon Banks (that save)

A stretch of lightning
the arc of triumph
beneath the unblinking sun
before the unbelieving eyes
between the gasps of hearts
turned sinew and muscle
through the air into legend
as the man
with certainty absolute
. wheeled away
body flexed in celebration
and yet
the prize already denied
as far-flung fingers
agile and alive with athletic dignity
pushed through a universe
of impossible angles
and the man
who was hero
paused
for just one
modest
breathless
moment of relief.

Catherine Marshall
Liverpool

Semi-Final 1978

Close quarters around the radio,
We listened in church-silence
To the troughs and peaks
Of the commentator's voice
And the sudden surges of noise
That hinted at distant glory.

One step away from Wembley:
Crammed even tighter
Around the kitchen table
Cradling cups of tea
As security blankets
(For once, ignoring the temptation
To take the mick out of Gary's twitch
Or Steve's B.O.).

Goal!
The fever-pitched cries
From the radio
Sent chills down our spines,
The illusion of Wembley
Snatched away
Like a jilted sweetheart.
All that early possession
A false dawn for what was to follow.

At the final whistle
It was like we'd been there -
It was us walking, disconsolate, from the pitch
Muddied and blooded
United in defeat,
Indolent in despair,
No clichÈs left in us.

Next season, lads, someone piped up,
There's always next season.

Andrew Detheridge
West Bromwich Albion

The Scottish Junior Cup Final

and it's doun tae
Cumnock Juniors and Auchinleck Talbot
in the final
an it's no jist anither gemme.
for the supporters
it's High Noon
it's showdown at the OK Corral
and for the players
it's time for an early bloodbath.

and we're standing on the terraces
singing
Away the 'Nock, Away
and shouting
and cursing
at everything and everytime
Talbot get the ba'.

It's do or die
and Cumnock's yin doun
wi five minutes left on the clock
- no counting injury time -
so that's another twenty minutes, easy.

It's life or death
then the Talbot do the dirty again
and score
a shite goal that was a mile offside
the chant goes up
bastards bastards bastards
and the pies fly
and the fists and the feet and the teargas
and it's enough to make you greet
When oot the blue
it's in the net, the Talbot's
a divin heider
and there's time left yet
for a miracle
you can feel it in your bones
a silence fa's ower the ground

then his cross gets turned intae a goal
and it's kill or be killed
as another player is stretchered aff.
then there's a player that's been asleep
for maist o the gemme
a flash o genius
an he's away up the wing
like a man possessed.
his cross hits the crossbar
thunders doun and crosses the line
Cumnock supporters' erupt
Talbot's shut up

the time ticks away
aw the supporters stay
then a wild tackle in the box
results in a penalty kick.
and suddenly it's two each

and it's mebbes aye and mebbes naw
it's unbelievable but it's for real,
when the wee winger goes and scores the winner -

And we are sailing
Sailing across the water
Stormy water...
Just to see you...

the final whistle blows.
and we'll aw be fighting in the streets o Cumnock the night.

John McCaughie
Cumnock Juniors & Ayr United

The Game, Or is It?

The game has gone from strength to strength
Even now reaching unknown depth and length.
Or is it just a game we play,
Only to while the time away?
Both men and boys expressing joy,
Showing off to the girls on the side
Puffing up with pride
As they score a goal.

Despite the constant falling rain
And howling in pain from a foul again.
yet bravely we play on. I mean what can you do?
The girls on the side are watching you.

I love the game
But it's just not the same.
Certain ones come to the grounds
Causing trouble, milling around,
Ugly racist comments,
Designed to disillusion and discourage.
How these things can weigh you down.

But is this game just a game,
Or does it have a greater claim?
Football has a language all of it's own
That has to be used and made known.
Football has surpassed creed and colour
And has so much more to offer.

For football, international barriers have come down
People have come from all around.
Let's use it to bring people together
Maybe to make a better future.

John Fashanu
England. Aston Villa & Wimbledon

Famous Player

Larger than television
he'd drink anyone
under the floor,
gathered around him
like family and fire,
waiting on every word
the smell of scandal
stronger than draught beer:
a holiday and setting fire
to women's knickers
the team behaving just like
any other slobby trippers,
obsessed with the size of plonkers
and dubious strikers
who could go either way.

The chairman's an asset-stripper
the manager's his dummy,
but he's City till he leaves
to sell his kicks
across the market-fields.
He talks fan lingo,
he was there when it "went off"
at Bristol, as though
the fighting was a bomb
someone else had planted.
He's liberated then bigoted
spitting "bent" and "racist"
in a single sentence,
shrunk in his shoes
we just begin to argue
as he gets up to go.

Mike Jenkins
Cardiff City

Journeyman Pro *(for Warren Aspinall)*

A familiar face we notice once a year
When, for the other side, a player appears;
Division 3. Is it him? How many teams?
Torquay? ....QPR? ...How it might have been.

Twenty-two he was; scouts sagely in the stand,
Old and wise as owls to feast his skills first hand:
He burst, he tackled, dummied, nutmegged, dribbled,
As knowing eyes watched on, busy hands scribbled -

It only took one tackle from the back
To lay him flat. Of course the man in black
Brandished instant red, not that cards mattered
At twenty-two with ligaments in tatters.

A whole year out, a comeback in reserves,
Orient away - is that what he deserved?
He looked up to where the scouts with pens were poised:
Silent seats, cold echoed rows. No crowd nor noise.

This season must be his last; he cannot take
The pace now, just 20 minutes as sub late
On. Next season? No media job, no fuss,
Just choice of vehicle: van or bus.

Thank God you see the humour in this game:
70 minutes gone ...Tannoy ...your name.
Less hair, more weight. Last time, you smile.- we cry:
"You ate all the pies, you ate all the pies."

Steve Driver
Burnley

Knackered Knee

"You've got an ulcerated bone where the tibia meets the femur."
"What's that mean then?"
"It means you'll never kick a ball again, son."
"What, no more lying horizontal to the Earth's surface,
Three feet in the air,
And scoring with a flying volley?
No more flinging your coats down on the ground
And arguing whether it's in or hit the post?
No more of that embarrassing jumping to head the ball
With your eyes closed?
No more chesting the ball down
And moving inside the full-back
With one sinuous movement?
No more being picked first?
No more trying to impress the girls on the touchline
By wearing your shirt outside your baggy shorts?
No more raising your arm aloft,
Fingers clutching your cuff,
Just like Denis Law?
No more creasing your brow
And shouting, 'How long to go, ref?'
No more bringing your muddied kit and boots home,
For your poor exploited mum to clean?
No more baggsying to be Bobby Charlton?
No more endless childhood
And infinite immortality?

Stuart Butler
Swindon Town

Physio's Lament

It's not much fun being a physio
at a high profile club.
Sometimes you come close to thinking,
Take me off, and bring on a sub.
When the queue for the treatment table
Stretches out into the street.
You're treating one player and
Musing, Who's the next skiver I'll meet?

When they come to me after surgery,
Some players have had their legs plastered
The language they use comes from playground
Ouch! Oof! You're a bastard.
It's not a ten grand a week job
Physiotherapy's not over priced
Most players sound so religious - well
They keep shouting, Oh, Jesus Christ!

It's not much fun being the Physio
To put right the club's damaged joints.
So I practice my specialist knowledge
To help the team win bonus points.
I don't win a big trophy,
a medal or a shield;
My satisfaction is to see my ex-patients
Run out onto the field.

Graham Shaw
Huddersfield Town

By the Waters of Liverpool

So many of her sons drowned in the slime of the trenches
So many of her daughters torn apart by poverty
So many of her children died in the darkness
So many of her prisoners slowly crushed in slave - ships
Century after red century the Mersey flowed on by -
By the waters of Liverpool we sat down and wept

      But slaves and the poor know better than anyone
      How to have a real good time
      If you're strong enough to speak
      You're strong enough to sing
      If you can can stand on your feet
      You can stomp out a beat...

So we'd been planning how to celebrate
That great red river of Liverpool
As our team rose to a torrent
That would flood the green of Wembley
We'd been planning how to celebrate
The great red dream of Liverpool
For Dalglish held the cup in his left fist
And the league in his right-
By the rivers of Liverpool we sat down and wept

Our scarves are weeping on the gates of Anfield
And that great singing ground is a palace of whispers
For the joy of the game,
Yes the great red heart of the great red game
Is broken and all the red flowers of Liverpool -
By the waters of Liverpool we sat down and wept.

April 1989 - Hillsborough
Adrian Mitchell
Liverpool, Scotland & South Africa

Wrigley Man

We watched him on the telly
At the Man United game,
He's their soccer manager
Sir Alex is his name.

He stands there in his box
And watches, as they run
But whatever is he eating
It must be Wrigley's gum.

He seems to enjoy this chewing gum
He chews at every match
And the cameraman is looking on
As he pauses, just to watch.

He's hooked on one big flavour
And his face is all aglow
When Beckham takes it up the line
And Roy Keane scores a goal.

When Man United miss a goal
His cheeks begin to drop
And until they start to play again
The chewing has to stop.

Then up and down they go again
To his teeth it won't be gluing
As these United players
Will keep our Alex chewing.

I don't watch a lot of football
But my husband is a fan
Of Manchester United.
And me - the **"Wrigley Man."**

Monica Mills.
Manchester United

Andres Escobar

The World Cup in America, Nineteen Ninety Four
USA- Colombia, do you recall the score?
And over in the Rose Bowl, the fever's running high
Colombia were on a roll, the moment it was now
their road would be to glory, to sweet success somehow.
I speak of Andres Escobar, I shudder at his name,
the linchpin in a strong defence and known throughout the game.

They called him caballero, the football gentleman
in soccer crazy bars and homes and right across the land.
In front of ninety thousand fans, Colombia v the States
the stadium heaved to anthem songs, behind the long closed gates.
The minutes gone were thirty-three, Colombia's stubborn wall
is broken by a hopeful cross, it looked like Andres' ball....
but as he stretched to intercept, the ball spun fast away,
it clipped his boot and in the net it landed on that day.
An own goal of extreme bad luck, the sorry deed was done
and one that proved to be his last, Colombia lost 2 -1.

Their World Cup dreams now over. Disaster in one game.
While friends stood by
        a finger dark
           sought out
              the one to blame.
With Medellin's current murder rate some twenty fold a day
his only ever World Cup goal, would prove the price to pay.
Eliminated, they returned to jeers instead of praise
and Andres' goal cost him his life, within the next ten days.............

July the First, a night club, where high up on a hill
they shot him like a dog that night, Escobar lay killed.
"Own goal-own goal," they shouted, as he sat in his car.
At point blank range, six times they fired, outside The Padua Bar.

On Medellin's streets they argue still on such a way to go,
a hit man or a drunken rage but we will never know.
A country rife with drugs and guns, so meaningless and sad.
"How can there be," his father cried, ìsome people quite so bad?"
"That they would kill my gentle son, that they his life could take,
all for a moment in a game - all for but one mistake."
And now while politicians and drug-lords wine and dine,
the coke cartels and 'hit men' come thick at any time.
Think then upon the price of life, the money and the dream,
those sexy football lifestyles aren't always what they seem....
and on those dusty pitches on Sunday you can see:
by breeze block slums, with washing hung, the dream of breaking free
and still they talk of that World Cup and of the fateful day
when Escobar stretched out too far, against the USA.

Crispin Thomas
Chelsea

George Best at Fifty

We have been estranged for many years
but spent your birthday weekend together
thanks to BBC2.
I toast you with a bottle of beer.
We agree on your finest goal.

I loved you with a tomboy's passion
mesmerised by your feet;
the left you worked and worked
with a tennis ball
until it obeyed with all the ease
of your natural right.

Your feet were part of my salvation,
lifting my spirit way beyond
the outstretched hands of blood - stained saints.
Watching those feet,
keeping my eye on the ball,
I dodged the defenders of the faith
left them standing, navy blue veils
blowing in the wind.

Saturdays I wore by brother's cast - off
Stylo boots, your name scrawled on the side,
and screw - in studs. The laces were so long
there was an art to tying them that boys knew.
I learnt the underneath and round,
the tying of the final, unflamboyant bow.
I was like you then;
flying down the wing, ball glued to my feet,
my brother's friends saying
"That's never a girl"
As they failed to stop me..

You were working class and and gifted,
uprooted, getting drunk, just like my father.
I prayed your name with others I collected;
all exiled Celts, the worse for drink
but worthy of respect. George Best
I'd say and Richard Burton, Richard Harris
covering the mouthpiece
when my grammar school friends phoned
so they wouldn't hear him shouting in the background.

Nell Farrell
Eastwood Town & Arsenal

Journey of the Maggies

the voices singing in our ears, saying
that this was all folly..- T.S.Eliot, Journey of the Magi.

A long, cold journey we had of it,
just the worst time of the year
for an away game at Barnsley,
the train packed, the weather lousy,
rain turning the snow to slush,
cops at the station
feeling bloody - minded
and answering no questions.
If we had any brains at all
we would be back home in the pub
shuffling the cards, and lining up the pints,
eyeing the women showing it off
at the bar, dressed for the pull.

Frozen stiff, we legged it
through that desperate town,
all of us cursing because of the cold,
the cost of the tickets and the cans.
I swear God invented away games
to punish us for loving football.
Then we spotted the floodlight gantries
silhouetted against a weeping sky,
hurried past the dirty pubs
full of our supporters ready to mix
it with the nervous natives.
Finding the right entrance, at last,
we knew this, and only this.

three points would send us to heaven,
make the tedium and the cold
a price worth paying for our journey.
Losing was like death, and we had died
too many times over the seasons
when the championship was ours for the taking.

All this was a long time ago,
but I would make the journey again
just to see the goal we scored
against the run of play, laugh
at the torments of the Barnsley crowd
dying the death of the relegated.
I can still hear our lot punch the air
with their obscene Songs,
knowing that a good run
would send us flying up the table
to the very edge of promotion.
We prayed for it night and day.
For the Premier League we would endure
all the winters in all the Barnsley's
of the far North, and beyond.
We dreamed of nothing but the vision
of a beautiful game played beneath the stars.

Derrick Buttress
Nottingham Forest

Where Were You

Where were you when Kennedy was shot?
         In the Second Division.
Where were you when England won the World Cup?
         Winners of the old Second Division.
Where were you when Armstrong walked
         on the Blue Moon? F. A. Cup Winners.
Where were you when City dropped to the second?
         'ead in me 'ands at Stoke.

I never will forget the sense of disaster
another horror story with City chapter.
the love of my life,
(no! not the wife)
singing the Blues
with the Blue Moon singers win or lose.
With the scally City fans harum-scarum
showdown at the OK Britannia Stadium.
Stay up or stay down
laurel wreath or crown (of thorns).
Radios tuned in to Bradford and Huddersfield.
First Division or Macclesfield, (Moss Rose).
Lancashire lads in Yorkshire hands or
it's off to foreign Second Division lands,
a point too few
or three points and...

Where were you when we won Five - Two
and still went down.

Ralph Hancock
Manchester City

It's Enough To Make Your Heart Go..

Woah.
A rush usually reserved
For those on the dance floor at Cream.
The roar, the Z-Cars theme
And the inevitable loo roll thrown on the pitch.

Previously.
The solitary march around the ground.
Gwladys Street to Bullens Road
And through the Park End Box Office.
Dodging Police horses and the kids asking
'Any spares mate?'

Now.
With a dodgy colour photo copy
Of the prototype Puma strip on my desk,
I realise that the tower, the laurel
And the badge itself
Have come to mean much more than most people
Would ever understand.
It's enough to make
Your heart go.

Andrew Taylor
Everton

Earache

If considering wearing an earring
But ear - holing might be too fierce,
Listen to Channel 5 football,
Get an earful of Jonathan Pearce.
You'll forget all about the needle,
It won't bother you much at all,
You'll have had both your ears 'Pearced'
By Channel 5's 'voice of football.'

He'll tell you with feverish excitement
The history of Northampton Town,
How many times East Fife have gone up
And how many times they've gone down.
He's a mine of rare information
A talking bookcase of stats,
He'll tell you the names and the ages
Of Keegan and Ferguson's cats.

And the things that make him go frantic,
That well nigh make him bust a gut:
How can anyone sound so passionate about
A back - pass from young Nicky Butt?
One night he went almost bananas
Which, in some circumstances is fine
But this was to tell us that Chelsea
Had a throw - in near their own line!

Soon he'll be joining us poets,
I've a feeling he's nearly ready:
On the replay of Sheringham's last televised goal-
He screamed, READY ...STEADY ...TEDDY!!!!
I don't wish this on football coverage
But Channel 5 this is your fate:
'For those who are hard of hearing-
Subtitles on page 888.

Graham Shaw
Huddersfield Town

A Poem of Two Halves.

(Gillingham v Sheffield Wednesday)

In the first half we done good
Just like I knew we would
Got a nice rhythm going
The lines were flowing
And we rhymed as well we could
With our pin point passing we had alliteration
The ball running at our feet - that's personification
When we tackled like lions, we managed a simile
Out of our skins we were playing hyperbole

But in the second half
The rhyme fell apart
And we never looked like metaphoring.
We went down to a last minute clichÈ
And were sick as parrots
It was an open secret about the way we felt
About the oxymoron who scored.

John Coldwell
Gillingham

Derby versus Liverpool

It was
I suppose,
A trip back to the future;
We travelled on an ancient Virgin train,
Rocking and rolling up the Lickey Incline,
Coffee spilling through the redbrick cowls and scowls
And warehouse development
Of the service-sector-
Prefab-English Midlands;
Until we met Alistair
At the prefabricated Derby Railway Station.
He placed a couple of bets
And then we walked out into Station Road,
Past the chip shops and pub,
("Open all day, special ales and international lagers,")
And past the Victorian railway cottages,
Until we reached the triangular Brunswick Inn;
Here,
Opposing fans drank in beery communion,
And here,
In the fag filled family parlour,
Pictures of Derby Railway works
And steaming seeming innocent goods trains,
Running through May blossom cuttings,
In 1920s' livery,
Reflected back the the Railway Terrace street sign,
Which stood opposite the window,
On the other side of the autumn sunny street.

We all chose our lucky scores,
50p in the family sweepstake,
And then we made our way to the football ground,

Through what were once the marshalling yards
Of Derby Railway Station;
No more fights,
No more running battles,
Just some ritualistic Scally bashing,
("Sign on, sign on, with hope in your heart,
And you'll never work again;")
We walked past the players' expensive cars,
With their personalised number plates
To enter Derby Football Club;
Derby Football Club,
Where men drink in the bar below the stand,
The bar laconically marked "BEER,"
The bar where men smoked fags and sank pints
And watched the game on telly,
Having paid twenty quid for the privilege
Of not having to watch it on telly;
Back to the future at Pride Park;
Who says modern life is rubbish?

Stuart Butler
Swindon Town

Le Match De Jour

It was an historic weekend in Llanthony Priory:
Because we played football with a stone,
In a lane, just like the Bisto kids,
And because I played football with a dog called Darcy,
(A reference to Pride and Prejudice,
Rather than to Arnold,
The fleet footed Swindon winger of the 1950s)
And because a fellow camper loudly declaimed that
"When I clean this frying pan,
I see the face of Zinadine Zidane,"
And because I recalled John Motson saying
That France's victory
In the World Cup 98 was the greatest night in Paris
Since the Second World War,
Only to be corrected by Emmanuel Petit,
Who said it was the greatest night since the Revolution.
And now these revolutionary principles triumph again,
iLiberte, Egalite and Fraterniteî on the football pitch
Make the ball mightier than Le Pen,
For freedom of expression and movement
Make both a society and a football team;
Citizens!
Thuram from Guadeloupe! Zidane of Algeria!
Desially! Lizarazu the Basque!
French footballers who trace their roots to Argentina!
Armenia! Ghana! Khazikhistan! New Caledonia!
Vive la Republique cosmopolitan et multiculturale!
Vive Ante - Fascisme! Vive Anti - Racisme!
Allez Les Blues!

Stuart Butler
Swindon Town

Retail Park Plaque

Below lies the body of the Goldstone Ground
Covered by contempt and never found.

Frank Cole
Brighton & Hove Albion

"Going to the Match"

An awfully puny figure!
1.7 million? - Hardly so!
Reminds me of the starving poor, or famine victims:
happier though.
Only hope he's worth it:
That's a fair amount of dough.

December 1999.
Done the deal at last: signed up on the dotted line.
Scrapbook of the past.
Not the same today: about as different as can be.
P.F.A must wait till April
for the move to Salford Quay.

Sotheby's were glad to have him.
Call that going for a song?
Underneath the hammer.
But not for very long!
West Ham can't compete: it's Lowry
draws the crowd and beats the drum.
Hope they weren't misguided.
Still can't believe the
sum...

There's no art in football:
has to be a catch.
Think of all that money
just for 'Going to the Match.'
Maybe there's a ray of hope.
Could have bought a centre-half
rather than a famous painting.
Almost makes you laugh!

Maybe this millennium
things are going to change.
Good to see the P.F.A. promoting art.
It's really strange:
maybe there is art in football...
Glad they've made a start
to put the record straight
and prove the game's a work of art.

Carolyn King
Ipswich Town

"Going to the Match" by L.S Lowry can be seen at The Lowry Centre,
Salford Quays, (Manchester).

I Have a Dream

I have a dream.......about a football team
                wearing shirts of royal blue
                Who win the League
                Who win the Cup
                Who conquer Europe too.

The team of the Millennium!
But will my dream come true?
                My team you see, is Everton,
          ....So much dreaming still to do.

Roger McGough
Everton

Inversely Reformed Character

'Who do you want to win, dad?'
Our Nicky once asked me.
'The team that deserves to,
So let's just wait and see.
As long as it's worth watching
And played in a good sporting spirit,
I hope the side that wins the game
Deserves to win on merit.'

But
That was several years ago
When I was less devotional,
Before I became over emotional.
For nowadays, I'm in a sensational
Blue and white stripped cult.

Do I give a fig for football?
No........Just a good result:
Very boring one nil wins
Will do very nice for me.
At the end of the season
They'll fill my heart with glee.

Bore me stiff - Town, Town - doze me off.
You'll still make this fan's tail wag
If by the end of this afternoon
You've put three points in the bag.

Graham Shaw
Huddersfield Town

M.P's 4 Football Manager 1
" a politician's arse upon which a man never sat."- e.e cummings.
who never used capital letters or full stops

well politicians, i never liked you,
and the fourteenth's events compounded that view

what, prithee tell me,what gives you the right
to use your positions to employ your might -
to, with no sign of nutmeg, subtle chip or lob,
try to put someone out of a job

gang of four, your treatment of wednesday's boss,
left me at a loss?
blunkett, ashton, michie and betts,
you ought to be suffering heartfelt regrets
for the treatment you recently metered out,
the way you tried to abuse your clout
and the way you betrayed wisa's trust
you should feel deep remorse, if not, self disgust

you must envy your manager and long for his cool,
football's no time for a corporate fool
a plea from me on behalf of the nation,
stick to messing up health and education

to imbue you with dignity should be one of my missions
but i'd have to abort it...........
                        as you're all politicians.

Graham Shaw
Huddersfield Town

Groundhoppers

When I was just a nipper I confided in my dad
"I want to be a groundhopper
It isn't just a fad."

He looked at me in disbelief "Oh, where did I go wrong?
I thought you'd follow Liverpool!"
He pondered all day long.

He said you'll need an anorak, a plastic bag and cap,
A pad to write your memoirs in,
A rail pass and a map."

I set off on my travels and hopped onto a train.
My first stop was at Daisy Hill
I braved the wind and rain.

I hopped across the Pennines to Pontefract and Goole.
Then travelled South to Tadley Town
To see their game with Poole.

I ventured on the Northern Hop,to Morpeth Town and Crook,
Then Jarrow Roofing BCA
(- I wrote these in my book).

I scribbled down team changes,when every goal was scored
And added up attendance's
Whenever I was bored.

I noted every blade of grass and never gave up hope
Of measuring geometrically
Which way the pitch would slope.

So next I'm off to Cornwall, to Launceston and Saltash,
But I'll have to get back home soon
As I'm running out of cash.

I've used up twenty Biros and filled three dozen pads.
My friends think that I'm crazy
-But I'm just groundhopping mad!

Barry Lenton
Marine F.C

Leigh Railway Mechanics Institute

Lost in a concrete jungle
And yet I feel so free,
For every fan has so much space
On a moon that some call "Leigh."

I miss old *Planet Horwich*
With its craters and its slope,
We'd struggled running up it
But our crampons gave us hope.

We'd ski between the goalposts
When it snowed before a game,
And speculate how railwaymen
Had formed its silly name.

Now Grundy Hill is flattened,
The sale invested well.
They've signed up loads of players,
Their massive squad to swell.

They've settled in the Conference,
And they've not let it down,
But don't you think that it is time
That somebody told the town?

Their average gate is minus ten
And that includes three dogs,
A pussy that's called RMI,
Some earthworms and two frogs

But things will change, just mark my words,
The crowds will flock to see
A team of stars that shines like gold
On a moon that some call "Leigh."

Barry Lenton
Marine F.C

Minute's Silence
(for Christopher Loftus & Kevin Speight)

We knew you just as images and names.
For you and those who love you, now we stand.
No more the giddy thrill before the game:
A tidal wave of sickness drowns our land.

A country sickened, silenced. Families weep
For two who died. It could be you or I
Whose innocent blood dyes the Turkish streets:
Wrong place, wrong time. So sadly such was life.

The Valley. Twenty thousand on our feet,
All corners of our stadium stand to stand.
Players linked in chain around the circle meet
In mind two men who never shook our hands.

The gates of Elland Road lie wreathed in flowers.
We bow our heads in deference to you,
Arms behind or front or side, all eyes lowered:
Red and white of Charlton, Town's white and blue.

Only turnstiles ticking in the wind sound now,
Silent seconds before the whistle's cue:
Go, lads, and play this game with heads unbowed
With fire and pride : for football.
Just for you.

Steve Driver
Burnley

The M4 Derby

August 19th 2000,
Listening to Radio 5,
Walking along the old country branch line,
And looking forward to Reading versus Swindon
And our first win of the season,
Until the radio described it as "The M4 Derby."
The M4 Derby?
Christ-
Whatever happened to "The Biscuitmen versus the Railwaymen"?
Where are the names and games of yesteryear?
Tempus fugit
And focus groups
I suppose;
And so I wander through the incomprehensible
Timetable of baffling change,
Evident from my headphones
And the landscape in front of me.
Old engine sheds,
Broken brick permanent way huts,
Mouldering sleepers,
A rusting fishplate,
Flowers in season,
Verdigris ferns,
Swallows flying high,
a haunting undertow of whistle, piston, rhythm,
Power and momentum,
A rash of needles, syringe, cans, glue and graffiti.
Tempus fugit;

Once it was a fag and Health and Efficiency,
Now it's shooting up and the Internet.
Once it was "The Biscuitmen versus The Railwaymen,"
Now it's the "M4 Derby."

Stuart Butler
Swindon Town

the ghost of Stanley Matthews

late in the game when the fog swirls in
and you long for the rub of the dice
you pray that some figure will dance through the mud
and cause havoc under the lights -
for legends and myths are like rivers
but there's one that will last for all time
and i swear that i've seen him appear through the mist
drifting like smoke down the line

and some here among you will nod and agree
and to some it is nowt but the same
but the ghost of sweet Stanley Matthews
still hovers around this great game -

Yes i swear that the ghost of Sir Stanley
still lingers on many a ground
with his bright orange shirt and his parting
when footballs were heavy and brown
yes i've seen him at Wembley, at Stoke and at Ayr
on muddied old parks coming out of thin air
just ghosting past players as if they weren't there
for he had a class so refined in his time -
and when i look out on some cold cold day
in a fifties and throwback and sad kinda way
i can still see him swerve i can still see that sway
for Stan was an idol of mine and so fine -

and maybe his shorts did come down to his knees
and maybe his hair was all Brylcreemed in grease
but there ain't a crowd that our Stan didn't please
but he's left us and gone now   long gone......................

and he probably went home with tuppence a week
for all that he did for the game
but he stood for a time and a working man's sport
that is sadly no longer the same -

but his ghost lingers on in the good things
whatever wherever they are
and i dare you to try and compare him
for Stan was a true soccer star

and some of you out there will nod and agree
and to some 'tis nowt but a name
but the ghost of sweet Stanley Matthews
still hovers around this great game

Crispin Thomas
Chelsea

Wembley

Abide with me, fast falls the eventide;
The crisis deepens o'er the national side.
Keegan has gone, successor's yet to be,
What's worse, they're pulling down our Wemberley.

Millions of fans have walked up Wembley Way,
To cheer their teams each year in early May;
Music and marching by the Guardsmen's band,
Chants only soccer fans can understand.

Out on the wing, Stan Matthews' artistry
Helped Blackpool win the cup in fifty - three:
Powers of destruction, though they do their worst,
Cannot erase the hat-trick by Geoff Hurst.

Fearful of failure, hopeful of success,
Through smiles of joy and tears of bitterness;
In life's perspective soccer's just a game,
Triumph, disaster - treat them both the same.

New stadium soon shall like a phoenix rise,
Where now twin towers point upward to the skies;
Though hearts may break, still football shall endure,
Dear Wembley, we shall love you evermore.

Geoffrey V. Willis
Ipswich Town

F.A.Cup Fourth Round Draw

Tension in the studio
Tension in the house
Who do City play next round
A lion or a mouse?
I pray for an away game
As funds are running low
It costs a ruddy packet
For all of us to go.

Well now we know.
At home again
Late January game.
So win it; - then get drawn away,
My pocket howls in pain.

Roy Butler
Manchester City

Dusk at the Welfare Football Field

Shapes in the gathering dark;
Ball a full moon.

Shouts across the welfare field;
Ball a tossed coin.

Cries as the dark gathers;
Ball a vague shape.

> 'These kids are the future, that boy there
> had scouts from all over looking at him,
> all over...

Hope on the dark field;
Ball a ticket out.

Shapes by the streetlight;
Ball under one arm.

> 'They'll come back when they are famous.
> Come back and help us, I know they will...'

Ball a tossed coin.

Ian McMillan.
Barnsley F.C.
Poet in residence

David Beckham

The man
in the fisheye lens
who plays with the
warmth of the son
on his back.

Dennis Bergkamp

Vincent's heir
who produced
the same swirling
colours of genius
with palettes of
living limbs
upon a canvas
made of grass.

Catherine Marshall
Liverpool

MUFC

Please.

I am not English
I am Man. Utd.

English is meadow.
A diaphanous glade.

I am scrub grass
& moor. Red.

Other.

Steven Taylor

I'm Only here 'Cause of City

I cannot wait for the Human Genome Project
to prove that City are in my genes
that I am City ''til I die
that I have blue
genes.

Ralph Hancock

the lads and a beer
(for Mike Scott/The Waterboys)

football was my first love and it will be my last
I would have loved to play for England but I was too crap to ask
it started in the playground and ended up in tears
so I'm sat here in the pub with the lads and a beer

Pele was my idol he was on my wall
I used to think I was Brazilian ev'ry time I got the ball
Jimmy Greaves and 'Bestie' didn't quite compare
but they wound up down the pub with the lads and a beer

Southgate broke my heart when he missed that penalty
if he hadn't lost his bottle we'd have beaten Germany
now we've got a pop - star captain and a Swedish 'mana-geer'
but I watched us beat them five - one with Sven and a beer

Wembley was a dream in every football town
I used to pray one day we'd get there now they're gonna knock it down
I don't know where they'll build it - and I don't really care
cos I'll be watching England for the price of a beer.

I used to go to matches and stand there in the rain
singing dodgy anthems we were not ashamed
now it's champagne in glass-boxes on the second tier
So we watch it all on Sky for the price of a beer.................................

we used to feel connected we were working class
we used to know the players but that's all in the past
the beauty of a live game is just too dear
so we watch it on the big screen for the price of a beer

we used to teach the children to play the people's game
now it's ruled by money and everything has changed
now it's just the rich and famous playing over here
and the kids are down the pub with the lads and a beer

so my story's almost over the memories are gone
but I'm still a football poet and football will go on
I don't know where it's going and I don't really care
'cos I'm going down the pub with the lads and a beer.

Crispin Thomas
Chelsea

Talk it Up

So there I am right it's nil, nil with ten
minutes left to go, I trap the ball dead
swivel round and weigh up the options. "Send
it, send it, " Baz is shoutin', "On me 'ead,
on me 'ead," screams Chopper, while the coach from
'r touchline's urgin' me to, "Go inside,
go inside," which is diff'rent to the man
with the dog who's yelling, "Come wide, come wide."
Time's runnin' out though, their right-full-back's bin
told to 'ospitalise me, bring me down,
an' not takin' to 'is mean toothless grin
I choose route one quick and go it alone.
The ball's like an extension of m' leg
as I move up-field ridin' one...two...three...
nasty tackles from their side and nutmeg
'r number nine who's cryin', "Give it me,
give it me you greedy bastard." By now
I'm on the edge of the eighteen yard box,
m' 'eart's pumpin' fast as the action slows
down an' I carefully tee up m' shot.
An' that's when it 'append, that's when it all
went pear-shaped. M' knee seized up, cramp struck, stitch
set in, hamstring snapped, laces broke, the ball
bobbled an' I shinned it, slewed it wide, missed.

Pissed in the bar later we go over
an' over each move again. A beer mat
an' a sleever form two goal posts either
side of a matchstick keeper. Mike "the Cat"
Brown's a prawn cocktail crisp, Tom's a Twiglet,
Dapper Payne's a Whatsit, I'm a pickled
egg and the ball's a dry roasted peanut.
After two or three hours we're ahead
by the same number of goals as pints we've
sunk - clear through this time to the County Cup.
an' as we finish off get ready to leave
I seize hold of my chance to talk it up.

Paul Newnham
Bristol City

Coventry City F.C. 2001

I entered the elevator
still clad in my sky-blue

the operator stared at me.
'Going down?'

I paid his hospital bills.

Ronnie Goodyer
Coventry City

distant fan

it was long ago before satellite dishes when tvs weren't even around
and videos weren't invented and only film hire shops down-town
and i was this far off supporter with two little kids and a wife
i was so far away but connected it was still such a part of my life..
cos when you've been smitten you follow your team-and you do it however you can
and when life gets too much well you still keep in touch that's the way of ev'ry day distant fan
and the scores come a day late in 'papers
it's weird when you wade thru the stuff
like problems and stress in Botswana
to find that your lads did enough
but at three ev'ry week i would be there
all of those long miles away
i'd be glued to that radio out on some beach
and i'd try to imagine the day...
like the snow as the sun would be baking
and the fog as i lay by the sea
the taste of the ice beer inside me
while longing for strong English tea
so you close up your eyes and you picture the scene
and the game's going on in your head
you're a long-distant fan by the ocean
and you wish you were back there instead
yeah it's strange when you're in some hot country
with a voice shouting loud in your ear
"were joined by our listeners from over the seas"
and you wanna shout "yes mate-i'm here!"
and 'the Final' was always a nightmare
a hundred degrees maybe more
some dirty old sheet and the dust from the street
and projectors that broke when they scored
there'd be prostitutes, ex-pats and waiters
and everyone crammed in the same

there'd be a whole tribes of Zulu's down at the front
who were there 'cause they just loved the game
and nobody asked you to do this no one but you wrote the plan
nobody else, apart from yourself is to blame for your plight distant fan

and here we all are in two thousand and one
and wherever you go it's the same
in a cafe in China or Cape Town
you can still keep in touch with the game
you got messages texting the planet
you got internet access all day
you got digital sound and ni-cam surround
and live interactive replay..
and whether you're broke or Elton
or that Damon bloke out of Blur
if you're Rod flippin Stewart or still signing on
well now you can watch anywhere-
if you're up in the Mad Dog on Haigh Street
in San Fran at dawn by the bay
or stuck in the Duke in the middle of Stroud
it's ok you can all find a way
cos when you've been bitten you follow your team and you do it however you can
and when life gets too much you can still stay in touch-that's the way
it's ok distant fan

Crispin Thomas
Chelsea

Scarcely Poetry

It was an extraordinary decision,
given that Sturridge
was not denied his scoring chance,
but Mr Dean was doing his level best
to appear decisive
and the error was carved in stone.

The crowd,
with every justification, erupted in anger.
Suddenly
   the air was full of Charlton merchandising
                  catalogues which had been left
            hopefully on every seat.
       They fluttered
   from the stands and littered the pitch.
     The match was halted
          as ground staff
             and coaches
         Gathered
       Great handfuls of
     Glossy brochures.

In more volatile arenas,
the fans would have hurled
more substantial ammunition.
No matter.
It was, quite possibly, the nearest thing to a riot
that this peaceful football corner of South-east London
had ever known.

Patrick Collins
Charlton Athletic

Postmortem

It was a game of two halves
And we were crap in both of them,
We reflected
Blowing the froth off our pints
In long, dejected sighs.

If only we didn't have a defence
As watertight as the 'Titanic'
Or a striker
Who couldn't score in a brothel,
We'd be one of those quality sides.

After rearranging beer mats
Into 4-4-2 formations
(And then heatedly debating
The value of wingbacks)
We trudged home through the snow,

Mulling over whether the same talk
Took place in bars from Barcelona to Milan.
(But they wouldn't have just lost
At home to Crewe
- so the answer's probably 'no').

Andrew Detheridge
West Bromwich Albion

Thanking the Monkey

ITV Digital
Was going to be pivotal
Football would have it all
The future was bright.
ITV Digital
Would give clubs the wherewithal
The players would have a ball
Long into the night.
ITV Digital
Would be inspirational
Its coverage invincible
All the leagues and the cups.
ITV Digital
Would be so sensational
Demand, so insatiable,
Would never dry up.
But ITV Digital's
Take-up was rather small
Too few would make the call
For a box or TV.
'Foul play!' cried the smaller clubs
When ITV pulled the plug
And then snatched away the rug
So cold-heartedly.
No squat knitted monkeys
Could turn football junkies
Into digital flunkies
There's no substitute
For watching your team
Pursuing their dream
In the flesh - not on screen -
Don't forget your grass roots.

ITV Digital
Saw many stocks take a fall
Backs are against the wall
But it's not just about shares.
It's about passion and pride
And supporting your side
To make sure they survive...
And showing you care.
Has ITV Digital
Done some good after all?
As Nationwide clubs now crawl
Back from the brink?
Players earn an honest crust
No team has yet gone bust
One day one surely must
So let's stop and think.
ITV Digital's
Demise was historical
The reaction hysterical
All sides lost their shape.
ITV Digital
Left football with bugger-all
But what a wake up call:
What a lucky escape.

Grahame Lloyd
Lincoln City

It Was

It was ... Action
It was ... Speed
It was ... Triumph
It was ... Adrenaline
It was ... Glory ...

It was ... Pain
It was ... Aching
It was ... Frustration
It was ... Depression
It was ... Rejection ...

It was ... FOOTBALL !

Gordon Taylor
Everyone,
with a close affinity
with those he played for.

Arsenal Double - 2002

Seaman, Wright and Taylor,
Did their job in goal,
A mixture of experience
And a youth called Ashley Cole.
Pires was mercurial,
Campbell always steady,
Loads of goals from Henry
And a Swede called Freddie.
A squad with so much talent,
Wenger should be knighted
And what a way to win the league,
At Manchester United.
A magnificent season,
Only three times saw defeat.
Chelsea beat in Cardiff,
Another Double was complete.

David Thrilling
Aston Villa

The Full Backing of the Board

Despite the dreadful run of recent results
Culminating in that 8-0 thrashing,
The manager still retains the boards' full backing.

Notwithstanding the anger of the fans
(Or the ongoing players' strike)
We will not be asking the Boss to take a hike

Let me reiterate - the manager is here to stay.
(Yes, we have considered our plummeting share price
And the sordid allegations of beneath-the-surface vice).

The players must stand up and take their share of blame
(Despite the startling slump in match day attendance's
And the revelations concerning the Boss's alcoholic tendencies).

So gentlemen of the press, thank you for your time
Do we need to spell it out to you any more?
(Oh, Boss, before you go, could you hand your keys in at the door?).

Andrew Detheridge
West Bromwich Albion

The Manager's Chant

At the end of the day
We should have won
At the end of the day
Football is fun
At the end of the day
They scored more goals
At the end of the day
Our best player must be sold
At the end of the day
We had no luck
At the end of the day
I couldn't give a ****
At the end of the day
There'll be night
At the end of the day
We just didn't fight
At the end of the day
We played like clowns
At the end of the day
The sun goes down
At the end of the day
I'm the one to blame
At the end of the day
It's only a game.

Mike Jenkins
Cardiff City

The typist

The typist who is a poet herself, stops typing my poems
in order to watch the World Cup.

Ted Booth
Charlton Athletic F.C.

The Underdogs

The football world drew its breath,
World class players selected
But many of the score lines were totally unexpected

From day one of the tournament
The mighty began to fall,
France the reigning World Champions were shocked by Senegal.

Ireland nearly said to Spain,
"Adios Amigo,"
Portugal went out early - Bye bye Luis Figo.

U.S.A a great surprise,
Japan played without fear
And Totti and Vieri couldn't stop South Korea

But the best of all was the "Group of Death,"
A roller coaster ride,
Argentina sent back home
As Batistuta cried.

Patrick Vieira
Patrick Vieira a star with the ball
How ironic it is, he comes from Senegal.

David Thrilling
Aston Villa

England 1 Sweden 1

Sorry, no poetry here

Argentina 0 England 1

A poor performance against Sweden
Dented morale within the squad
But the next game saw revenge
For the ìHand of God.î
After his red card in St. Etienne,
No player was much keener
And David Beckham kept his cool,
Don't cry for me Argentina.

England 3 Denmark 0

World Cup favourites were homeward bound
As our Lions played the second round.
Against France, the Danes were tasty,
Like their bacon and their pastry.
But England blew them off the park;
Rio got us off the mark,
Five minutes gone, hearts a flutter,
Sorensen's fingers just like butter.
A quarter-final did await,
as Beckham began to create,
from right to left he did roam -
Owen coolly slotting home.
England strolling, the Danes had gone,
An occasional threat from Thomasson.
Gronkjaer, Romedahl used their pace
But Mills and Cole won the race.
Hesky celebrated with his DJ jive,
After netting the third with a right foot drive.
Such a mountain for the Danes to climb,
It wasn't even yet half time...

It was never going to be a rout,
The second half calmly played out,
England 3 Denmark 0.
Bring on - bring on Brazil.

Brazil 2 England 1

(Seaman's Hell)

A Brazilian named Ronaldinho
Dealt England such a huge blow
From forty yards out
Shot or cross is in doubt,
Where the hell did Seaman go?

David Thrilling
Aston Villa

Super Ireland

Yet another great World Cup; a memorable Irish story
As Mick McCarthy and his men covered themselves in glory.
Not without controversy, the lead up was all doom,
But the smiles came back, after the draw with Cameroon.
Team spirit was immense, the fans a sea of green,
The hero against Germany was a Mr Keane.
Not Roy, the captain, sent home in disgrace,
But a Robbie equaliser, brought delight to McCarthy's face.
Staunton won his 100th Cap. Two points on the board,
Nothing less than a two goal win, could his men afford.
In the next game versus Saudi, that goal from Gary Breen,
Secured the win required. *who needs Roy Keane?*
The first target was accomplished, in a group that was so tough
A star in the making shone; Blackburn's Damien Duff.
A sloppy goal conceded in the second round -
Spain, one of the favourites but the Irish did astound.
They missed a penalty but deserved to win
And finally equalised, after a foul on Niall Quinn.
Golden goal extra time, the Spaniards just sat back,
Ireland bombarded them, with four players in attack.
The shoot out ended their quarter final dream
Vital spot kicks missed - Holland, Connolly, Kilbane
The Irish dream was over, no final in Japan.

David Thrilling
Aston Villa

Samba Champs

In South American qualification,
They struggled - couldn't score,
Just scraped into fourth place,
Even below Ecuador.

But come the World Cup finals
With flair, imagination and pure skill,
Typical Samba style,
Under a coach they called "Big Phil."

Ronaldo, Ronaldinho, Rivaldo
What a great attack,
With eighteen goals and seven wins
Brazil won the trophy back.

David Thrilling
Aston Villa

Zinadine Zidane

Besieged those
sun-kissed hearts
baptised in the
January river
the post modern
architect wrapped
in the tricolour
where Le Foot
is mightier
than Le Pen.

Catherine Marshall
Liverpool

Meet The Players

Ted Booth: age 64, married, played parks football till 47 for the worst
team in London. Ex University lecturer and beer drinker, still a regular at
Charlton, revelling in their success in the Premier League.(with fingers
crossed). His book, *First Draft* sold many copies and has only a few left.

Roy Butler: life long Man City fan, who finds the strain of supporting the
Blues a drain on his pocket and emotions but still goes with his family.

Stuart Butler: played football for Swindon boys, later a founder member,
with Dennis Gould, of the Stroud Football Poets; bringing arts into the
community. Major contributor to www.footballpoets.org.com. A charis-
matic performer who reached a poetic Cup Final reading football poems at
The Royal Festival Hall. Recently made Deputy Sheriff of L.A.P.D. for
anti-racist poetry work.

Derrick Buttress: is addicted to tobacco, poetry and Nottingham
Forest F.C. Still dreams of their past glories. Written drama for BBC 2 &
Radio 4 & has broadcast on Radio 4. Prize winning poet with poems
published all over the place. Has been writing them for so long he says
he's forgotten why he writes poetry.

Frank Cole: stimulated to write about Brighton approaching their 100th
year in 2001 and their moving around the south of England. His poems
have appeared in the Brighton fanzines and the match-day magazine.

Patrick Collins: Columnist for The Mail On Sunday with an honest &
clear perspective on the attributes and eccentricities of football. He
describes the extract from his column as 'scarcely poetry.' *'But it is
definitely poetic.'* - Ed.

John Coldwell: Schoolteacher and performance poet, with 100s of
published poems in his trophy cabinet. Author of the humorous
children's poetry book *The Slack Jawed Camel-* (Stride Books)
Devon EX1 2EG.

Andrew Detheridge: one of the prominent poets retained from F:PP *(1)*.
Now dominating the small poetry presses, sometimes with a selection of
his poems in consecutive issues, winning a few prizes en route. Known as
Bard of the Baggies from his poems in Grorty Dick, fanzine at WBA. Also
MA in English communications and poet in residence at Sandwell
College, W. Mids. Clear to read and totally relentless.

Steve Driver: 'Minute's Silence' is adapted from his original and commissioned for this book & has been on display at Leeds United F.C.
His first book *Electric Poetry!* for schools displays his command of poetry styles and is enhancing his reputation in Lancashire. But can he get football on the National Curriculum? Steve is still hopeful of making his debut for Burnley F.C at the age of forty six. *See his poem in Football: Pure Poetry (1).*

Nell Farrell: lifelong fan of Eastwood Town in the Unibond League and proud to witness their first entry into round 1 of the F.A. Cup. She also contributes to their programme. Nell is a massive Arsenal fan *(but don't tell, as this is no way for an East Midlands girl to behave).*

John Fashanu: Ambassador of Sport for Nigeria & UNICEF is an eloquent and tireless worker for the underprivileged. Capped twice for England, ex - Wimbledon and Aston Villa forward. Presented *Gladiators* for ITV. Now specialises in introducing Nigerian footballers into the Football League via his Winners World Wide (Sports).com Ltd.

Dennis Gould: founder member, with Stuart Butler of Stroud Football Poets. Played football for the Army & Newbury Town, later qualified as a coach & referee. Founded Whisper & Shouts: Riff Raff Poets (1968 & 70) Performer & organiser of poetry at colleges, clubs & festivals since 1964.

Ronnie Goodyer: an established and popular poet, so afflicted with Sky-blueitis he used to dream of Coventry F.C. season tickets when living in Greece. Now in the West country enjoying the fresh air.

Ralph Hancock: Man City season ticket holder. His poem '228 2255' in F:PP *(1)* was recorded by Greater Manchester Radio for the Jimmy Wagg programme and an astonished Ralph listened to himself on the radio as he drove to the game. Latest book: *Hermit Space - A Journey Through Uncertainty.* ISBN 1 899114 71 8 - (Spout Pubs), is a search for answers in an uncertain world. Only £6.00

Seamus Heaney: a Danny Blanchflower of poetry; both leaders, using their skills with intelligence, economy and imagination. Author of more than twenty books.Professor of poetry, working in Ireland and the U.S. He was awarded the Nobel Prize for Literature 1995.

Mike Jenkins: an avid Bluebirds fan and accomplished poet who has written a nine poem sequence on City. His latest books are *Could Bin Summin* (Planet) and a short story for children, *Barbsmashive* (Pont)

Carolyn King: Isle of Wight poet and consistent Ipswich Town F.C. supporter. The only woman to be retained from F:PP (1). Winner of the Hastings International Poetry Prize (2000) and twice Island winner of the Ottakar / Faber Prize. Her latest collection is Lifelines ISBN 0953186016

Barry Lenton: The Unibard Poet and supporter of Marine F.C. can be spotted ground hopping around the Unibond League writing his clear & imaginative odes about the non-league clubs.

David Longley: from a long standing, and sitting, family of Turf Moor season ticket holders, he remembers the day Burnley stars John Connelly & Ray Pointer scored the goals for England to qualify for the World Cup in Chile. Looks forward to his sons & grandchild enjoying similar successes.

Grahame Lloyd: Cardiff based freelance journalist, has commentated & reported for BBC, HTV. Works for *Rothmans Football Yearbook, uefa.com & Nationwide Web Page, The Guardian & occasionally The Independent. Author of One Cap Wonders,* (Robson) *Jan the Man,* (Gollancz), the life story of Jan Molby. *C'Mon City!* (Seren), Cardiff City's official centenary book.

Catherine Marshall: loves Liverpool F.C. Penned as Parry Maguire she wrote Beautiful Game, (Slamdunk)'A Jules Rimet of football poetry;' high-lighting players from Florian Albert to Dino Zoff, stars from the 40s to today. She has published three children's poetry books, which with her *Box of Dreams* is in schools in 26 countries. Cathy has been Awarded UNICEF Cultural Contribution Award 2003 (China).

John McCaughie: often writes in dialect and arguably the best poet, ever, reared in Cumnock, Ayrshire. He grew up to be a supporter of Cumnock Juniors, with a hatred of the other local team, Auchinleck Talbot. Transferred to Edinburgh where he is involved in writing & performing poetry & prose. Sadly the Hibs v Herts derby is friendly compared to Cumnock v Auchinleck.

Roger McGough: Everton fan-Liverpool poet who burst into the Poetry Premier League with Brian Patten and the late Adrian Henri as part of the famous Liverpool inside trio. Making the Under 23s Hit Parade with The Scaffold. Took Europe by storm with more than 20 collections. Like Hughie Gallagher, Matthews or Best, who sent opponents in the opposite direction, Roger does similarly but takes you with him. Awarded OBE in 1997.
www.rogermcgough.org.uk & www.uktouring.co.uk

Ian McMillan: took football poetry to prominence with his book, *It's Just Like Watching Brazil.* A popular poet, broadcaster, commentator and programme maker for T.V. and radio. In constant demand yet still finds time to write for the *Guardian & Mail On Sunday* More at ***www.ian-mcmillan.co.uk & www.uktouring.org.uk***

Monica Mills: writes poetry for pleasure and it's also her pleasure watching her husband enjoying Manchester United on T.V. as often as possible in their home in Co Down.

Adrian Mitchell: was born in London,1932. Poet, playwright & author of children's stories. Developed an interest in football while working at the Liverpool Everyman Theatre, becoming an armchair supporter of Liverpool, Scotland and South Africa. '*By The Waters of Liverpool*' published in Blue Coffee - Bloodaxe Books. Most of his poems can be found in *Heart on the Left* also from Bloodaxe.

Paul Newnham: Bristol City supporter,who "was there! to witness their unenviable first." Their fall from Div. 1 - Div. 4 in consecutive seasons in 1979 - 82. Paul is a "Poetry Activist" operating from a Central Midlands Library.

Gareth Owen: has had four poetry collections & six novels published. His first football poem was *Denis Law* in the 60's. Gareth has presented Poetry Please! on radio 4. Everton fan.

Graham Shaw: the bard of McAlpine Stadium,'Towns' official poet often tours as The Blackcurrant Jelly Brothers duo, entertaining adults and children with poetry and song. His *Scwank,* Rogue Gene Pubs, explores bawdy humour in the style of the travellers & jesters of the Middle Ages. *I'm Pink Therefore I'm Spam,* is a collection of his observational rhymes.

Ted Smith-Orr: Played football for West Wickham F C, in the Southern Amateur League. Proud to have seen both of Charlton F C 7 - 6 victories, v Huddersfield and Sunderland. Organiser with Poets Anonymous, Croydon. He has read in pubs, clubs, theatres and a tent in a field,and poetry venues from Edinburgh to the New Forest. Interviewed and read on radio stations including the BBC. Looks forward to going to bed before 3.0am.

Andrew Taylor: is a life long Evertonian. His poems have been published nationally in print, and on the airwaves. His poem was published in the Everton Fanzine, *When Skies are Grey*. Poet in residence at Liverpool Architecture and Design Trust and a volume of his poems is due out 2003.

Gordon Taylor: played for Bolton, Birmingham, Blackburn Rovers & Bury, also Vancouver Whitecaps in the States. 1972, joined the P.F.A Management Committee, including Terry Venables & Bobby Charlton, succeeding Derek Dougan as Chairman in 1978. Chief Executive 1981. With the demise of I.T.V Digital, Gordon & the P.F.A are busy helping players & clubs.

Steven Taylor: born & brought up in Hyde near Manchester, now lives in Kilburn, north London, as the Man Utd aspect of a Liverpool supporting Irish family. Steven is widely published in many good mags & journals and is currently assembling his first collection of poems. A version of his poem appeared in *Global Tapestry*.

Crispin Thomas: active member of the Stroud football poets and www.footballpoets.org His *'Out to Lunch'* poetry band has appeared at many Theatre's & festivals around the country. Humorous, socially and politically aware with a great stage presence. Although Crispin has read his poems around the world, he has only recently been published.

David Thrilling: lives in Greater London where he is player manager of Talksport F.C. A season ticket holder at Aston Villa, having been born and brought up in Birmingham. David dreams of possessing the talents of Paul McGrath and Gordon Cowans, and would love to get rich, buy all the tickets at *Birmingham City* and never turn up. *We are grateful to him writing verse on our request. Thanks - Ed.*

Geoffrey V. Willis: has been married to Jean for forty one years, they have two sons and four grandchildren. Since being introduced to football by his son Andrew, then aged seven, Geoffrey has become a season ticket holder at Portman Road. He has been writing poems since 1988, working hard to have them regularly accepted by the programme at Ipswich Town. F.C.

WEBSITES

Barry Lenton plus: **www.marinefc.com**

Ian Macmillan: **www.ian-macmillan.org.uk**

Roger McGough: **www.rogermcgough.org.uk**

www. footballpoets.org Dennis Gould-Stuart Butler - Crispin Thomas - Detheridge - Shaw - Smith Orr & loads more has been called the best football / poetry web site in the world.

Andrew Taylor **www.andrewtaylorpoetry.com**
   "   "   **www.ladt.org.uk**
Crispin Thomas **www.ctmk.com**

Essential Reading:
Football
Grahame Lloyd, *One Cap Wonders,* Robson. Settle some of those arguments about who played only once for UK countries.
Jan the Man, Gollancz. A big story about the big man, Jan Molby.

Mike Jenkins, *C'Mon City*, Seren. 100 years of Cardiff City. Official.

Catherine Marshall (as Parry Maguire) The Beautiful Game, Slamdunk Books. £8.40. Beautiful poetry on the beautiful game.

Poetry:
Derrick Buttress, *Waiting for the Invasion,* Shoestring Press. Clearly written and entertaining read, giving insite into life around the 30s. Born into a working life and digging himself out to become a Headmaster and writer of renown. One of a fewl collections.
Ted Booth, *First Draft,* Yew Bears Press, 49 Achilles Rd, London NW6 1DZ. £5 A retrospective worth buying just to read the outrageous 'Wallasey Climbing Club' poem - a ritual to send you racing up a mountain!

Other Books from Creative Energy Publications

Charlton Athletic Poetry in Motion. One fan's account,
in verse, humour, comment and poetry, of the famous Play-Off-Final
against Sunderland at Wembley 1998 .Good press and
Radio.Commended by Bob Murray, Chairman of Sunderland FC.
Reprinted in 2001. £4.50 ISBN 0 9534296 0 1.

Football: Pure Poetry. *(for the fan who wants everything).*
Collection of poems from fans of football and poetry from around the
UK. Includes Ian MacMillan, Roger McGough & Brian Patten,
& many others. *"A labour of love for a year."* Croydon Advertiser
"Football is such an emotive subject it is perfect for poetry."
Birmingham Evening Mail. Read at festivals and BBC Radio 2,
London Live, GMR & 107.5 £6.99 ISBN 0 9534296 2 8.

Forthcoming title:
West Bromwich Albion, Pure Poetry. Featuring Andrew
Detheridge, (ìthe Bard of the Baggiesî) and others. If you can
remember the days of Ray Barlow, Ronnie Allen and others up to the
seventies and would like your poems to be selected for this collection,
please forward your poems to our address.